Central Florida Home Renovations, LLC...

A

Journal

Just For You

Sign Up For Your 10
FREE
Printable Mandala Coloring Book Pages Now!.

Check Us Out on Social Media
Email: michael@liveasuperchargedlife.com
https://www.facebook.com/liveasuperchargedlife/
https://www.instagram.com/liveasuperchargedlife/
https://www.youtube.com/channel/UCwfgl-GmDbQf5C0m7bLEiUQ
https://www.pinterest.com/liveasupercharg/
https://twitter.com/Superchargedway

Check Out Our Other Books
https://www.amazon.com/author/booksbymichael

http://www.liveasuperchargedlife.com/books-by-michael/

Check Out Our Other Books

This Book Belongs To

Central Florida Home Renovations, LLC

Name: _____ Date: _____

Address: _____ Room: _____

Phone: _____ Notes: _____

Central Florida Home Renovations, LLC

Name: _____ Date: _____

Address: _____ Room: _____

Phone: _____ Notes: _____

Central Florida Home Renovations, LLC

Name: _____ Date: _____

Address: _____ Room: _____

Phone: _____ Notes: _____

Central Florida Home Renovations, LLC

Name: _____ Date: _____

Address: _____ Room: _____

Phone: _____ Notes: _____

Central Florida Home Renovations, LLC

Name: _____ Date: _____

Address: _____ Room: _____

Phone: _____ Notes: _____

Central Florida Home Renovations, LLC

Name: _____ Date: _____

Address: _____ Room: _____

Phone: _____ Notes: _____

Central Florida Home Renovations, LLC

Name: _____   Date: _____

Address:_____ Room:_____

Phone: _____   Notes:_____

Central Florida Home Renovations, LLC

Name: _____ Date: _____

Address: _____ Room: _____

Phone: _____ Notes: _____

Central Florida Home Renovations, LLC

Name: _____ Date: _____

Address: _____ Room: _____

Phone: _____ Notes: _____

Central Florida Home Renovations, LLC

Name: _____   Date: _____

Address: _____   Room: _____

Phone: _____   Notes: _____

Central Florida Home Renovations, LLC

Name: _____   Date: _____

Address: _____   Room: _____

Phone: _____   Notes: _____

Central Florida Home Renovations, LLC

Name: _____ Date: _____

Address: _____ Room: _____

Phone: _____ Notes: _____

Central Florida Home Renovations, LLC

Name: _____ Date: _____

Address:_____ Room:_____

Phone: _____ Notes:_____

Central Florida Home Renovations, LLC

Name: _____   Date: _____

Address: _____   Room: _____

Phone: _____   Notes: _____

Central Florida Home Renovations, LLC

Name: _____ Date: _____

Address:_____ Room:_____

Phone: _____ Notes:_____

Central Florida Home Renovations, LLC

Name: _____ Date: _____

Address: _____ Room: _____

Phone: _____ Notes: _____

Central Florida Home Renovations, LLC

Name: _____   Date: _____

Address: _____   Room: _____

Phone: _____   Notes: _____

Central Florida Home Renovations, LLC

Name: _____ Date: _____

Address: _____ Room: _____

Phone: _____ Notes: _____

Central Florida Home Renovations, LLC

Name: _____   Date: _____

Address: _____   Room: _____

Phone: _____   Notes: _____

Central Florida Home Renovations, LLC

Name: _____ Date: _____

Address: _____ Room: _____

Phone: _____ Notes: _____

Central Florida Home Renovations, LLC

Name: _____ Date: _____

Address: _____ Room: _____

Phone: _____ Notes: _____

Central Florida Home Renovations, LLC

Name: _____   Date: _____

Address: _____   Room: _____

Phone: _____   Notes: _____

Central Florida Home Renovations, LLC

Name: _____ Date: _____

Address: _____ Room: _____

Phone: _____ Notes: _____

Central Florida Home Renovations, LLC

Name: _____ Date: _____

Address: _____ Room: _____

Phone: _____ Notes: _____

Central Florida Home Renovations, LLC

Name: _____   Date: _____

Address: _____   Room: _____

Phone: _____   Notes: _____

Central Florida Home Renovations, LLC

Name: _____ Date: _____

Address: _____ Room: _____

Phone: _____ Notes: _____

Central Florida Home Renovations, LLC

Name: _____   Date: _____

Address: _____   Room: _____

Phone: _____   Notes: _____

Central Florida Home Renovations, LLC

Name: _____ Date: _____

Address: _____ Room: _____

Phone: _____ Notes: _____

Central Florida Home Renovations, LLC

Name: _____ Date: _____

Address:_____ Room:_____

Phone: _____ Notes:_____

Central Florida Home Renovations, LLC

Name: _____ Date: _____

Address: _____ Room: _____

Phone: _____ Notes: _____

Central Florida Home Renovations, LLC

Name: _____ Date: _____

Address: _____ Room: _____

Phone: _____ Notes: _____

Central Florida Home Renovations, LLC

Name: _____ Date: _____

Address: _____ Room: _____

Phone: _____ Notes: _____

Central Florida Home Renovations, LLC

Name: _____ Date: _____

Address:_____ Room:_____

Phone: _____ Notes:_____

Central Florida Home Renovations, LLC

Name: _____ Date: _____

Address: _____ Room: _____

Phone: _____ Notes: _____

Central Florida Home Renovations, LLC

Name: _____ Date: _____

Address: _____ Room: _____

Phone: _____ Notes: _____

Central Florida Home Renovations, LLC

Name: _____ Date: _____

Address:_____ Room:_____

Phone: _____ Notes:_____

Central Florida Home Renovations, LLC

Name: _____   Date: _____

Address:_____   Room:_____

Phone: _____   Notes:_____

Central Florida Home Renovations, LLC

Name: _____ Date: _____

Address: _____ Room: _____

Phone: _____ Notes: _____

Central Florida Home Renovations, LLC

Name: _____ Date: _____

Address: _____ Room: _____

Phone: _____ Notes: _____

Central Florida Home Renovations, LLC

Name: _____ Date: _____

Address: _____ Room: _____

Phone: _____ Notes: _____

Central Florida Home Renovations, LLC

Name: _____ Date: _____

Address: _____ Room: _____

Phone: _____ Notes: _____

Central Florida Home Renovations, LLC

Name: _____   Date: _____

Address:_____   Room:_____

Phone: _____   Notes:_____

Central Florida Home Renovations, LLC

Name: _____ Date: _____

Address:_____ Room:_____

Phone: _____ Notes:_____

Central Florida Home Renovations, LLC

Name: _____ Date: _____

Address: _____ Room: _____

Phone: _____ Notes: _____

Central Florida Home Renovations, LLC

Name: _____ Date: _____

Address: _____ Room: _____

Phone: _____ Notes: _____

Central Florida Home Renovations, LLC

Name: _____   Date: _____

Address: _____   Room: _____

Phone: _____   Notes: _____

Central Florida Home Renovations, LLC

Name: _____   Date: _____

Address:_____   Room:_____

Phone: _____   Notes:_____

Central Florida Home Renovations, LLC

Name: _____ Date: _____

Address: _____ Room: _____

Phone: _____ Notes: _____

Central Florida Home Renovations, LLC

Name: _____ Date: _____

Address: _____ Room: _____

Phone: _____ Notes: _____

Central Florida Home Renovations, LLC

Name: _____ Date: _____

Address: _____ Room: _____

Phone: _____ Notes: _____

Central Florida Home Renovations, LLC

Name: _____ Date: _____

Address: _____ Room: _____

Phone: _____ Notes: _____

Central Florida Home Renovations, LLC

Name: _____ Date: _____

Address:_____ Room:_____

Phone: _____ Notes:_____

Central Florida Home Renovations, LLC

Name: _____   Date: _____

Address:_____   Room:_____

Phone: _____   Notes:_____

Central Florida Home Renovations, LLC

Name: _____ Date: _____

Address: _____ Room: _____

Phone: _____ Notes: _____

Central Florida Home Renovations, LLC

Name: _____ Date: _____

Address: _____ Room: _____

Phone: _____ Notes: _____

Central Florida Home Renovations, LLC

Name: _____ Date: _____

Address: _____ Room: _____

Phone: _____ Notes: _____

Central Florida Home Renovations, LLC

Name: _____ Date: _____

Address: _____ Room: _____

Phone: _____ Notes: _____

Central Florida Home Renovations, LLC

Name: _____ Date: _____

Address: _____ Room: _____

Phone: _____ Notes: _____

Central Florida Home Renovations, LLC

Name: _____   Date: _____

Address: _____   Room: _____

Phone: _____   Notes: _____

Central Florida Home Renovations, LLC

Name: _____ Date: _____

Address: _____ Room: _____

Phone: _____ Notes: _____

Central Florida Home Renovations, LLC

Name: _____ Date: _____

Address: _____ Room: _____

Phone: _____ Notes: _____

Central Florida Home Renovations, LLC

Name: _____ Date: _____

Address: _____ Room: _____

Phone: _____ Notes: _____

Central Florida Home Renovations, LLC

Name: _____   Date: _____

Address: _____   Room: _____

Phone: _____   Notes: _____

Central Florida Home Renovations, LLC

Name: _____ Date: _____

Address: _____ Room: _____

Phone: _____ Notes: _____

Central Florida Home Renovations, LLC

Name: _____   Date: _____

Address:_____   Room:_____

Phone: _____   Notes:_____

Central Florida Home Renovations, LLC

Name: _____ Date: _____

Address: _____ Room: _____

Phone: _____ Notes: _____

Central Florida Home Renovations, LLC

Name: _____ Date: _____

Address: _____ Room: _____

Phone: _____ Notes: _____

Central Florida Home Renovations, LLC

Name: _____ Date: _____

Address: _____ Room: _____

Phone: _____ Notes: _____

Central Florida Home Renovations, LLC

Name: _____ Date: _____

Address:_____ Room:_____

Phone: _____ Notes:_____

Central Florida Home Renovations, LLC

Name: _____ Date: _____

Address: _____ Room: _____

Phone: _____ Notes: _____

Central Florida Home Renovations, LLC

Name: _____ Date: _____

Address:_____ Room:_____

Phone: _____ Notes:_____

Central Florida Home Renovations, LLC

Name: _____ Date: _____

Address:_____ Room:_____

Phone: _____ Notes:_____

Central Florida Home Renovations, LLC

Name: _____ Date: _____

Address: _____ Room: _____

Phone: _____ Notes: _____

Central Florida Home Renovations, LLC

Name: _____ Date: _____

Address: _____ Room: _____

Phone: _____ Notes: _____

Central Florida Home Renovations, LLC

Name: _____ Date: _____

Address: _____ Room: _____

Phone: _____ Notes: _____

Central Florida Home Renovations, LLC

Name: _____ Date: _____

Address:_____ Room:_____

Phone: _____ Notes:_____

Central Florida Home Renovations, LLC

Name: _____ Date: _____

Address: _____ Room: _____

Phone: _____ Notes: _____

Central Florida Home Renovations, LLC

Name: _____ Date: _____

Address: _____ Room: _____

Phone: _____ Notes: _____

Central Florida Home Renovations, LLC

Name: _____   Date: _____

Address: _____   Room: _____

Phone: _____   Notes: _____

Central Florida Home Renovations, LLC

Name: _____ Date: _____

Address:_____ Room:_____

Phone: _____ Notes:_____

Central Florida Home Renovations, LLC

Name: _____ Date: _____

Address:_____ Room:_____

Phone: _____ Notes:_____

Central Florida Home Renovations, LLC

Name: _____ Date: _____

Address: _____ Room: _____

Phone: _____ Notes: _____

Central Florida Home Renovations, LLC

Name: _____ Date: _____

Address: _____ Room: _____

Phone: _____ Notes: _____

Central Florida Home Renovations, LLC

Name: _____ Date: _____

Address:_____ Room:_____

Phone: _____ Notes:_____

Central Florida Home Renovations, LLC

Name: _____ Date: _____

Address: _____ Room: _____

Phone: _____ Notes: _____

Central Florida Home Renovations, LLC

Name: _____ Date: _____

Address: _____ Room: _____

Phone: _____ Notes: _____

Central Florida Home Renovations, LLC

Name: _____ Date: _____

Address: _____ Room: _____

Phone: _____ Notes: _____

Central Florida Home Renovations, LLC

Name: _____ Date: _____

Address: _____ Room: _____

Phone: _____ Notes: _____

Central Florida Home Renovations, LLC

Name: _____ Date: _____

Address:_____ Room:_____

Phone: _____ Notes:_____

Central Florida Home Renovations, LLC

Name: _____   Date: _____

Address: _____   Room: _____

Phone: _____   Notes: _____

Central Florida Home Renovations, LLC

Name: _____   Date: _____

Address: _____   Room: _____

Phone: _____   Notes: _____

Central Florida Home Renovations, LLC

Name: _____ Date: _____

Address: _____ Room: _____

Phone: _____ Notes: _____

Central Florida Home Renovations, LLC

Name: _____ Date: _____

Address: _____ Room: _____

Phone: _____ Notes: _____

Central Florida Home Renovations, LLC

Name: _____ Date: _____

Address: _____ Room: _____

Phone: _____ Notes: _____

Central Florida Home Renovations, LLC

Name: _____ Date: _____

Address: _____ Room: _____

Phone: _____ Notes: _____

Central Florida Home Renovations, LLC

Name: _____ Date: _____

Address: _____ Room: _____

Phone: _____ Notes: _____

Central Florida Home Renovations, LLC

Name: _____ Date: _____

Address: _____ Room: _____

Phone: _____ Notes: _____

Central Florida Home Renovations, LLC

Name: _____ Date: _____

Address:_____ Room:_____

Phone: _____ Notes:_____

Central Florida Home Renovations, LLC

Name: _____ Date: _____

Address: _____ Room: _____

Phone: _____ Notes: _____

Central Florida Home Renovations, LLC

Name: _____ Date: _____

Address: _____ Room: _____

Phone: _____ Notes: _____

Central Florida Home Renovations, LLC

Name: _____ Date: _____

Address: _____ Room: _____

Phone: _____ Notes: _____

Central Florida Home Renovations, LLC

Name: _____ Date: _____

Address: _____ Room: _____

Phone: _____ Notes: _____

Central Florida Home Renovations, LLC

Name: _____ Date: _____

Address:_____ Room:_____

Phone: _____ Notes:_____

Central Florida Home Renovations, LLC

Name: _____ Date: _____

Address: _____ Room: _____

Phone: _____ Notes: _____

Central Florida Home Renovations, LLC

Name: _____ Date: _____

Address: _____ Room: _____

Phone: _____ Notes: _____

Check Out Our Other Books